Jeb Loves Bambi

Diane Marie

ISBN 979-8-89309-979-9 (Paperback)
ISBN 979-8-89309-980-5 (Digital)

Copyright © 2024 Diane Marie
All rights reserved
First Edition

All rights reserved. No part of this publication may be reproduced, distributed, or transmitted in any form or by any means, including photocopying, recording, or other electronic or mechanical methods without the prior written permission of the publisher. For permission requests, solicit the publisher via the address below.

Covenant Books
11661 Hwy 707
Murrells Inlet, SC 29576
www.covenantbooks.com

Living in the Midwest, out in the country, can have lots of wonderful rewards along with some trade-offs over city living. The dusty gravel roads are the thoroughfares that lead to the smooth pavement and town. The conveniences of city dwelling are forfeited for the wide-open spaces that give you freedom as well as room to move around and grow. Country living affords you a firsthand look at God's creation even at a distance. Each dawn and dusk, the fields are dotted with the white-tailed deer as they come out to graze. The countryside is filled with nocturnal as well as daylight inhabitants. It's like a peaceful coexistence between man and animals with our paths crossing on occasion. Some of those meetings do not end well, while others add richness to all of our lives. The story that follows is one in truth about such an encounter.

Mid-June was cooler and drier than usual. I was going to take my nightly four-mile gravel road bike ride that Thursday and expected it to be a very pleasant time for me and Jeb, our family dog. I had recently purchased my "new to me" Huffy bike at a garage sale and was very pleased with it. It was tan with brown trim and handlebars that came back to meet you, so you would not have to bend over to ride. Our youngest daughter calls these bikes the "Dorothy" bikes, for they remind her of the one in *The Wizard of Oz*, where Toto rode in the basket on the back. I like them because they are comfortable to ride. Jeb was eager to get started as he barked at the rolling front tire. He seems obsessed with that tire turning when we first start out but soon gives the barking up to jog alongside me.

After turning the corner just half a mile east from the drive, we headed north. The cool breeze blew over my face, and no bugs were pelting me. About half a mile north, we passed an old farm site that could probably tell many tales if it could talk. I always have wondered about who lived there and what their life was like all those years ago. Their view of the river was fabulous. But now things lay in decay with wildflowers, tall grass, saplings, and fallen trees filling in the spaces.

As Jeb jogged and I pedaled, we passed by the south end of the building site. I was looking at the cornfields taking in their beauty and fragrance. The farmers were

scrambling to get their irrigation pipe laid and flowing with life-giving water. The corn was somewhere between knee and waist-high with the ridges ready for the flow of water to give it that all-needed drink. I pedaled on, and as I passed the north drive, I looked down those first corn rows noting that every other row had water. The white pipe lay on the edge of the field and dirt drive. In the dry second row, there lay the teeniest, tiniest, itty-bitty fawn I had ever seen. The fawn was right up against the irrigation pipe looking all around. I grabbed my brakes and stopped to get a closer look. Of course, Jeb quickly found this little fawn there and jumped right in the row. He frightened the baby creature, and it flew up and ran into the field with him in hot pursuit. They ran about a quarter of the way down the row, darted across a couple of

rows, and then came barreling back and jumped the pipe. The fawn crossed the drive and dashed into the tall grass and trees in the abandoned farm site. Jeb was not letting it get away. As I called to him, he kept chasing, and I followed.

The fawn dove headfirst under a fallen tree branch with Jeb barking at the frightened little animal. The fawn lay there motionless as he circled. As I called Jeb off, he seemed to ignore my request. I reached down and pulled the fawn out and gathered the trembling baby up in my arms. I could feel its little heart pound so fast as it struggled in my grip. Jeb was jumping up and down, barking for this little life to play with him. We walked to the dirt drive out in the clearing to inspect our little bundle.

Jeb is an Australian shepherd, or better known as an Aussie. Aussies are herding dogs and love to have a job to do that entails chasing or herding or protecting. He is not really big, standing around seventeen inches at his withers. His color is tan, brown, and white swirled together with one blue and one brown eye. He seems smarter than his owners at times. At two years old, we have had lots of fun with him since he came to live with us as a puppy. Every time we do take him with us to town, horse shows, or visiting, he is always the center of attention. Most folks find that Aussies are wonderful dogs and want one just like Jeb. He represents his breed well as they are loyal and very protective.

Giving this little one a full inspection was the first thing I did. The navel was gone, telling me the baby was at least a week old, and the sex was female. As I held the fawn close to me, she leaned her little head into my arm. Her long thin legs were tucked under her little spotted body. Her ears were very alert. I had never held a baby deer before.

Jeb Loves Bambi

As her little heart stopped pounding so fast, I knew that I needed to place her in the tall grass for her mama to claim. We walked a short distance into the grass, and I placed her in a soft bed of green. She curled up and made no effort to run. Telling Jeb that we had to, he reluctantly followed me to the bike at the road as he looked over his shoulder. I had to pedal for home. Quickly, Jeb followed.

On the ride home, I thought it might be nice to get a few snapshots of this furry little creature of God's kingdom. If she was still there, I would capture her sweet image in film. Parking the bike in the garage, I raced into the house and grabbed the camera. Putting Jeb in the back end of the pickup, we drove over to see if the little fawn was

still in the grass. I really did not expect her to be there. Mr. Farmer had come to open up the gates on the irrigation pipe. We parked in the dirt drive and waved to him while he was working. As we walked into the tall grass, we found that little fawn, and she had not moved one inch. Jeb quickly wanted to play, and it frightened her. She jumped up and ran into the old building site again. Jeb was in hot pursuit with me in the rear. When the fawn was overcome with exhaustion and fear, she just dropped down and curled up. She lay motionless as I scooped her up and went to show her to the farmer. He thought she was really tiny. A few days before, he had seen just-born twins in the corn row on another farm. When born, fawns weigh from six to eight pounds, are covered with spots, and sleep lots. Finding my camera, I snapped a few shots. Then I thought it would be nice to show her to the neighbors up the road a short distance. So I put her in the front of the pickup, and she curled up on the passenger side on the floor. Jeb hopped in the rear as I dropped the tailgate. Knocking at the door of LaVern

and Shirley's, I was certain they would enjoy the opportunity to hold such a wee one. They took one look and fell in love too. Bringing out their camera, they too took several pictures of this tiny beauty.

Jeb patiently waited in the back of the pickup while we cooed over the bundle of fur, wide eyes, and large ears. When he could stand it no more, he jumped out and wanted to be close to the fawn. Startling her, she took off running into their tree line with Jeb right behind. I joined the chase and managed to grab her rear leg before she disappeared into the thicket. Carrying her back to the pickup, I knew then we needed to return her to the place where mom could come for her little baby. Snapping the last few pictures, Shirley waved goodbye, and we drove back to the old farm site down the dusty gravel road.

When I pulled into the dirt driveway, I tried to note if there was a mother watching in the shadows. Nothing I could see would tell me that, for there were just too many places to hide. We got out and again placed her in the tall grass, this time in a new spot. We said our goodbyes, turned, and walked away. Looking over my shoulder at her large eyes blinking, she seemed to be saying something I didn't understand or even want to think about. She lay there so brave, so alone, so small, and so still. We got back in the pickup and headed home. Jeb kept looking at her and seemed to be saying, *It's okay, I'll take care of you.* Now that's impossible, for he is a neutered male dog. But there seemed to be a word spoken between the two species. And I only could read the body language that evening as the sun sank on the horizon in the cloud bank.

After finishing up chores outside when we got home, I wanted to call it a day and headed to the house. I really wanted to see how the pictures of the fawn turned out as well. After turning on the computer in our office, I pulled the media card out of the camera and put it in the copy machine. Clicking enough buttons to bring up the photos, I could see that this little fawn was really special. I quickly sent the pictures over to our neighbors so she could share them with her family and friends as well. What an evening it had been. Locking the door, taking my shower, and crawling into bed, I wondered about that precious and defenseless little fawn right now. Would the mama be there by now, giving her supper and protecting her? Would she be scared of the animals that all come out at night? Would a coyote have her for supper? Or was her biggest fear, man, who was now far away from her little nest in the grass, gone for good? As I lay on my pillow, a million thoughts raced through my mind. Remembering the story of *Black Beauty*, I could almost hear that baby's thoughts of her evening encounter with Jeb and me. I could not get that wide-eyed, big-eared sweet little fawn out of my thoughts. In my mind, I put the mother doe near her baby, which gave me peace enough to fall asleep.

At first light the next morning, there was a welcome, slow, steady rain falling. It was good to hear the drops hitting the window and see the puddles in the yard. I decided to shower, have tea, and eat my breakfast before doing chores. The horses were getting that all-natural rainwater shower as they waited for me to bring them in for their breakfast. Keeping the show horses in the stalls during the day keeps them from getting too much sunshine, and putting them out at night gives them running time together. The horses seem to know the minute I step out the door, for they line up at the gate for their short trip to the barn. Jeb always helps me lead them in, for he grabs the lead rope with his teeth and pulls them toward the barn. He loves this job. He will also toss me his ball, so I will give it a kick, and he'll fetch it. He loves this game, and anyone who drives in will be asked to play fetch. If he cannot locate his ball, he'll settle for a stick. He is the perfect dog for anyone who never tires of fetch. However, this morning, he was nowhere in sight. I called for him in the barn, the garage, and the back shed. No Jeb. Hmm, where can he be? I finished up chores and decided that there were two places to look. First stop would be the old abandoned place where we left the fawn the night before.

Starting up the pickup, I turned on the wipers, which smeared bug guts all over, but in a short time, the windshield was clean. I drove down the wet gravel road to the dirt drive at the north edge of the deserted building site. Getting out of the pickup, I called to Jeb. He came bounding out of the grass, soaking wet. Jumping up and down, he wanted me to follow him to his little fawn. There she lay all curled up, perfectly dry. It appeared Jeb had returned to her grassy nest to spend the night with her. He was her protector from danger, from the weather, and even from mom. As I stood in the falling rain, I wondered what I was to do now. He would never leave her, and the mom would not return with him cuddled around her baby.

Quickly thinking this situation through, I knew that there were two options I could do. Under plan A, if I left that little fawn there in the grass, Jeb would not leave her side, and the mother deer would not return. The end of that plan would be a death by starvation for this white-tailed baby. So I opted for plan B and gathered her in my arms and went to the pickup. Jeb was thrilled and eagerly hopped in the back. He usually rides up front with me but willingly gave up his spot for this little one. As I drove down the road, I wondered what I was going to do. I had not raised a fawn before. I had no feeding equipment or milk. Baby fawn lay quietly on the floor, and Jeb peered in through the back window to observe his prize. First thing, she needed a name so I could reference her easily. Of course, it had to be Bambi. One thing out of the way. I drove to another neighbor's house. They had two small girls, and I thought that maybe, just maybe, she might have a suggestion for me as well as a bottle and some formula. And I even thought that she might like a little project for her small girls to be involved with. Last summer, they had found a fawn in the field and brought her home for a few days, after which they returned her to the field in hopes that mom would claim her offspring. They were expecting a new baby of their own, and bottle-feeding a fawn wasn't a task that would fit into the busyness of that.

As I drove up their half-mile lane, I somehow knew that Bambi's destiny was going to be with Jeb and me but thought that maybe our neighbors would like this little project. Shutting off the pickup and picking up Bambi, I went to the house to show the girls. They were thrilled to see and touch this sweet little baby. Katie was hurrying around the house doing early morning jobs; however, she was able to find a calf bottle with a small nipple. She put some powdered milk with warm water in it and gave it a shake. As we tried to see if Bambi would suck, her phone rang and a friend stopped by. Her life was filled with lots of activities as a farmer's wife; however, she really thought long and hard about keeping Bambi for the girls to help feed when I asked her. As I sat there holding Bambi, Jeb watched from the front door. In the end, it seemed right to take Bambi home and find a spot for her at our place. Bambi seemed less interested in the feeding, and so I took the bottle, her, and Jeb out to the pickup, loaded them up, and drove home.

Now where was I going to put her? It had to be a tight solid place, or she would be off and running. The shed behind the garage seemed likely; however, it was not escape-proof. This shed was where Chipper, one of our horses, stayed when bad weather blew in, so it was horse-proof. The horse trailer might do for a short time, but not long term. After

parking the pickup, I gathered Bambi up with Jeb in tow, and we went to the small shed. He wanted to keep watch over her, and I thought that would be just fine.

I went to the barn to find a small bale of hay to block any escape route under the door.

While in the barn getting the hay, Bambi and Jeb took off across the yard. Jeb was circling her every step until she darted under the electric fence and went into the stud yard. He stood there barking, knowing full well that yard was forbidden territory. Bambi just dropped down in sheer exhaustion. Coming from the barn, I saw the situation unfolding. I quickly went through the horse gate and picked her up before she got her second wind. Chipper, the palomino stud, stood and watched us racing around in the rain after this lightning-fast deer. He watched the deer travel by his yard every day as they move from one field to another. They have run into his fence, breaking some of the wires, and then bound over the ones remaining as they race for the river. He has even witnessed hunters putting their prize in their pickups when deer hunting season opens. I know he wondered what all the fuss was about as he watched us. When I walked by him, he sniffed my bundle and said nothing. Jeb jumped for joy as we came out of the yard and did a beeline for the shed.

Getting her settled in the little shed was the next action we did. Opening the door and placing her gently on the floor, she scampered quickly to the corner with Jeb right beside her. Seemingly a little frightened, she quickly laid down, refusing to budge. I called Jeb over to my side, and he watched her ever so carefully. Placing the hay bale under the door and then swinging the door shut, I found that was going to work perfectly. One problem: there was a space of about ten inches that the bale was too short for. Grabbing a bucket off the wall hook, I placed it to block the hole. Perfect, all looked right enough to hold a tiny little fawn. Seeing that she was laying quietly and watching us, we left the shed and closed the door. Now, I needed to find some of that milk replacer for fawns, goats, and the like. Off to town Jeb and I went to check out the farm store.

In my mind, I could almost see and hear on an island in the river standing in the tall grass was Bambi's mother watching the other does feeding their babies. The loss of her special little one seemed to make her the outsider. Only yesterday, like all mother does, she placed her wee one in a spot to stay safe while she went to forage for food. Did not her child listen to her command? Settling her deep in the cornfield for cover seemed to be the perfect spot for safety. Surely she would not have gone out to play without her okay. Then, she recalled finding her in the tall grass across the dirt drive with a new protector. How could she ever reclaim her fawn with this dog circling her child and cuddling it? Even when calling her baby to her, there was no way Bambi could respond. She appeared safe and in no danger, but she was held captive by the dog, Jeb. Watching was all she could do. Then there came that pickup and a lady calling to the dog. After a short time, they gathered up Bambi and put her into their pickup and drove away with her fawn. How sad and lonely she was for the newborn offspring. And just where could she be? Could she ever find her again? Would she be okay? With the falling rain, it seemed to add to her sadness as she thought about her loss.

The first stop at the local farm store proved to be the right place to go. They had a bucket of powdered milk just for such animals as fawns. So I picked it up and headed to the counter to pay. Placing the milk in the pickup where Jeb waited patiently for me and hurrying home made me happy to know I would soon feed this little fawn. When we pulled into the drive, the rain had nearly stopped, and a cool breeze seemed to blow part of the clouds away. I took the bottle to the kitchen and cleaned it up. Opening up the milk replacer bucket was like opening up a flood of memories for me. Years ago, on another farm in Iowa, we used to feed lots of baby calves, and I had mixed up lots of calf bottles. Those little black-and-white calves always latched onto the nipples and sucked until the white fluid was gone. They always seemed to want more. What fun it was to feed them twice a day. Now I was going to take on the job of rearing this little fawn. Dumping in a measured amount of powder and adding the warm water, it was easy to mix it up with a shake. Off to the little shed Jeb and I went. Would this little one take to a man-made bottle over mom? I guess I was about to find out.

Bambi was still curled up in the corner and was very wide-eyed when we opened the door. She lay perfectly still, for she had learned that lesson from her mom.

I opened her little mouth and squirted some warm milk into it. She seemed to wrinkle up her nose with the first taste and the rubber nipple. She popped up and then wanted to latch on to the meal. I held my hand close to her little nose and leaned her little head into my leg. Trying to be like her mom here was not fully happening, for she knew we smelled different, but her hunger kept her sucking. After about a cup of milk had been suckled down, Bambi pulled away, not wanting any more. I felt like we had gained a lot of ground in a short amount of time with this feeding.

Jeb licked her all over as to clean her up. It was so funny to see him mothering this fawn. He cleaned up her nose to her tail. What a dog. Now I knew she needed to rest. Making Jeb come outside with me was not to his liking, for he wanted to stay with her. I was sure she was not going to escape, and he followed me out.

After all of the morning's activities, I decided I needed a second shower after which I pulled on a robe. Sitting at the kitchen table sipping on the second cup of tea,

I glanced out the window. It had begun to rain again as the clouds thickened overhead. There, to my surprise, were Jeb and Bambi darting back and forth across the hayfield. She was trying to escape into the tall grass in the windbreak north of the house. Jeb was circling her to keep her from that destination. I quickly slipped on my shoes and charged across the field. That was a sight to see, me in my house robe, sneakers, and the rain falling. The two of them were darting back and forth as Bambi tried to escape, and Jeb tried to keep her from getting away. I called to Jeb, and he kept his eye on the task at hand. Finally, Bambi tired and dropped down to rest, which gave me the time I needed to retrieve her. Carrying her back to the shed, I was thinking that it was a great thing to have captured just when I did. I needed to secure the door a bit more. Jeb had pushed in to be with her and opened up that little space for them both to race across the field. Replacing things so neither one could push through seemed to be easy to do, but would it last?

Bambi rested, and so did Jeb. I redressed myself and got to the rest of my day, doing the things I put on hold while I tended to the care of the fawn. That night our youngest daughter was coming home for a weekend visit from the USAF. The next day, we were having a small family gathering with some friends bringing over their horses so everyone could go riding. Needless to say, there were many things to complete before the company did arrive. It would be good to have Danyal home, even if it was a short visit. When she drove in at midnight, I directed her to the shed to give Bambi her late-night feeding. She thought Bambi was pretty cute, and she suckled down several ounces of milk. We said our good nights and went to sleep.

The next morning, I had to drive about ninety miles to pick up our son for the visit, which left Danyal in charge of chores. During the drive home, Mark and I visited about lots of things. He was anxious to ride horses and have a cookout at home, and he had never seen a teeny fawn up close either. When we drove in the lane, I told him to go to the back shed, and there he would find Bambi. When opening the door, the place was empty. I was sure she could not have escaped, but she was gone. Jeb was laying in the yard, seeming unaware of her absence. I was so disappointed, for I couldn't begin to imagine where to look for her. Would she be okay? And now family and friends were not going to get to see her. We called for her and walked through the hayfield, but to no avail. It seemed that she was now gone for good.

Danyal was up in her room and had no idea that Bambi was missing. She said she was there when she fed her earlier that morning. It seemed that Jeb had pushed open the little space, gotten in with her, and let her out again. Everyone started to pull in shortly after we arrived home. It was time to get the grill warmed up for hamburgers and hot dogs and set the picnic table.

As I busied myself with all of the meal preparations, I could not get that little fawn out of my mind. The kids played fetch with Jeb, and he chased anything that they would throw. He was happy to have new ones to play with, never tiring out. We settled down to a great meal and ate too much. The horses were saddled up after dinner, and riding was the order of the rest of the afternoon. All too soon, the day was over, and everyone had to go home. By sunset, we were all tired, and I still wondered where Bambi could have taken off to.

The next morning, Danyal made plans to return to the Air Force base in Wichita. We ate a late large breakfast, packed her pickup, and said our goodbyes. I had laundry to hang on the clothesline, so I carried that basket up the stairs to go outside. All was quiet around the home place again, and Jeb lay in the yard looking toward the windbreak of trees. As I walked to the line, I asked Jeb where Bambi was. He looked at me with this smug look on his face as if to say, *Follow me*. As he ran toward the trees, he looked over his shoulder to see if I was coming. He jumped the fence and bounded through the tall grass to a spot. Then he came running back to me, barking. Following him through the waist-tall grass as he barked, I found that sweet little Bambi all curled up. Jeb was bouncing as if to say that he knew where she was all the time. It was a secret until things settled down at home. I picked her up to notice that she was really thin from not eating for over twenty-four hours. She didn't resist me much. Jeb was so happy to have her back in our possession again that he bounced all the way back to the shed. There, I quickly fixed her bottle, and she eagerly drank a cup of milk. When talking with my husband, he said that Jeb had not been there in the morning when he got up early. Surely he was out sleeping with Bambi until it was okay to bring her home again.

Several days passed, and Bambi was always ready to eat each time I entered her little shed with the bottle. I fed her four times each day. She seemed to be growing, getting stronger, and adding weight. I would let her out to run some with Jeb circling her so as to keep her from going too far. When she tired of his closeness, she dropped down and rested. He would place his paw on her so as to keep her from moving before he knew it. They jumped and darted around the yard in play. After I felt they had enough play, I would scoop Bambi up and place her back in her little home. She was always so good. It was easy to love such a sweetie. I could not help but wonder just what road this relationship would travel.

On a Wednesday evening after having her for less than a week, I was outside enjoying the beautiful evening. The night was so still, the sky so clear, and the lightning bugs were starting to light up across the fields. Out of the quietness of dusk, Jeb started to bark and chase something, for I heard thundering hooves. I ran to the east side of the house to see if the horses were out. But much to my surprise, he was in hot pursuit of a mother doe. She had wandered up near the house. It seemed strange, for she was by herself. I called Jeb back, and she ran into the hayfield, stopped, and turned to face us. As she watched us ever so closely, we watched her. I wondered why she was alone and so near. I ran into the house to get the binoculars so I could get a closer look. She circled around to the north side of the buildings, never seeming to be fearful. Then as the darkness drowned out my view, she walked away into the night. Could this be a mother looking for her baby?

Shortly thereafter, my husband came home, and I told him of the incident. We both wondered *if* this could be Bambi's mother. He went outside to check on things, and there, right by the garden, right by Bambi's shed, stood the mother doe. She jumped away into the darkness, only to return several more times. Could this be Bambi's mother? My mind could not even think of those thoughts. I had visited with the vet as well as many others who said the mother would never take her back. Once human scent is on their baby, they will deny them totally. So naturally, I was assuming that this fawn would have to grow up in my care until she could survive on her own one day. The thought of that day put tears in my eyes as well. What fun she was. We lay in bed that night wondering if this was a mother coming to claim her baby and if we should have let her go. My prayer was, *Dear Lord, if this is the mama, have her return tomorrow night, and we will then release her child*

The next morning, I hurried out to see if Bambi was okay and ready for her feeding. She popped up and stretched long and then turned to nursing her breakfast from the bottle.

She was a good little girl and somehow must have been more curious than she should have been that day we found her lying near the irrigation pipe. Jeb always jumped in and licked her from head to toe while she ate. He really loved this long-legged sweetie. She liked his attention as well. He made sure her face was clean after suckling, for not one drop of milk could be wasted in his mind. I had some errands in town that day and knew I would be gone for a little longer than the usual time between feedings. So before I left, I offered her an early lunch. She took a few sucks but really wasn't hungry. Saying goodbye, I went to do my business, leaving her to her cozy little spot till later.

It was later in the day before I was able to return home. I quickly mixed up her milk and went to feed her. She was ready to eat and sucked down over a cup this time. Jeb wanted to stay in the shed with her and clean her up. I let him do so as I tackled the horse chores. They were scolding me for being late and quickly inhaled their grain. After they had cleaned up every last crumb, I took them out to their pasture yard for the night. I then had to clean their stalls and get things ready for the morning. The sun was setting as I carried the last bucket of water. I went to let Jeb out so we could play a little fetch before dark.

As the hour of 9:00 p.m. passed, I went inside the house after scanning the hayfield and tree line to see if Bambi's mom was going to return. There was no sign of anything but the lightning bugs and late-night songbirds. Fully trusting that our Lord is a prayer-answering God, I did expect to see this searching mother deer return for her baby if, in fact, she was mom. It was only a matter of time.

I washed up in the bathroom and headed for the computer to check my email box. Just as I got things turned on, Jeb started barking wildly. What could have him in such a ruckus? I stepped out the back door and looked for any movement. Nothing could catch my eye. I returned to my desk, and Jeb again started barking loudly. I grabbed the binoculars and opened up the door, coaxing Jeb inside. Could Bambi's mom be out there somewhere? Jeb would not sit still and tried to push the door wide as I went out. I told him to go back and sit, and he obeyed. I quietly walked north to see if I could see anything. And sure enough, on the east edge of the tree line just northeast of the house stood a mother deer. She was watching me and did not turn to run. I peered through the glasses and could easily see that this was not a buck. I lay down the binoculars and quickly walked to the shed where Bambi had been living. Grabbing her up into my arms, I told her that her mama had come to take her home. She seemed to know that it was time to go. She gave me no struggle as I held her close and quietly walked to the edge of the hayfield. All this time, the big mother doe was watching us ever so quietly. Her keen sense told her to be patient. Jeb was barking wildly in the house, and I could not let him out, not even to say goodbye. I stroked her spotted fur and told her goodbye. She seemed to know it was time to leave. I placed her on the ground, and she jumped into a tall clump of hay that was as high as her. She then turned and looked at me with those big eyes and fully perked ears and stood and stared. She too was saying goodbye, and we held each other's gaze for a long moment. I then said "Shoo!" and waved my hands and said her mama was waiting. Tears streamed down my face as she turned and ran, hopping and darting toward the tree line. She had flipped her little white tail over her back, jumped over the low fence, and was gone.

My attention then turned to the doe. She stood ever so stately, watching this whole event. After Bambi had disappeared into the trees, the mama doe turned and slowly walked east away from the thicket of trees. Looking through the glasses, I could see that she had a full udder, and she did not flip her tail over her back and run. She just walked ever so slowly away. Not wanting to drive her away from her little fawn, I turned and went into the house to see how Jeb was doing.

Jeb had found a suitable place on the rug in front of the sink and popped up when I came in. He too seemed to know that Bambi went home to her mama. He howled at me, and I petted his soft fur and said he had to remain inside with me for a while. I shut off the computer and got ready for bed. Just before crawling under the covers, I let Jeb out. He immediately started barking, but I hoped by this time the reunion had taken place, and mother and child were long gone. Slipping into bed with the covers up close to my face, I thanked the Lord in my nightly closing prayer for sending Bambi's mom to fetch her and for giving me the strength to release her to her mama's care. Jeb stayed by the house most of the night, for I heard him barking off and on.

Jeb Loves Bambi

The next morning, things seemed a bit different at chore time. Jeb knew Bambi was gone and did not even race over to her door for feeding. We did the horse chores, and I did peek in the little building to find it empty. Asking me to play fetch with his ball, I threw it a few times. As sad as I felt about the departure of Bambi, I knew it was the very best thing for this little fawn. I guess it's the mother's heart in me that knew she needed her mother's care, and somehow Jeb understood that too.

The things I have learned from this encounter with God's creation are many. The lessons in this true story are clear. The Lord seemed to reinforce His order of creation that we sometimes take for granted. Even in the animal kingdom, parents love their children while sometimes the offspring fails to understand their commands. Learning to be thankful for all things that we get to enjoy seems to be something so simple that gets lost in our lives these days. It's not about the gathering of many items into our fold, but about enjoying each day and observing the many blessings that are around all of us. Stopping to watch the sunset, giving thanks for the songbirds that add music to our day, the smell of the falling rain, wildflowers and turned earth in the fields, as well as the touch of the grass and the soft fur of our pets are just a few things we are given to enjoy. Being a part of life and those things around us can bring great blessings if only we will look. All of creation displays His love and handiwork. We must be thankful for all the things the creator God has given us to enjoy. God hears and answers prayers even for the smallest of His creation.

About the Author

Growing up on a dairy farm in Midwestern America in the 1950s and '60s, I always had contact with God's creation. Milking cows and feeding baby calves was a hands-on lifestyle. We had baby chicks and laying hens, always a dog and cats plus farrowing hogs for those baby pigs. As the eldest of twelve children, there were many jobs for everyone. After high school graduation, I married my childhood sweetheart, and we were engaged in farming too. We had livestock as well, milking cows, feeding baby calves, foaling equine, raising hogs, and a couple of dog breeds for the sale of puppies.

Through the years, we always had animals to care for, giving you an understanding of how the mother of each species cared for their young. No one must teach that mama to care for her baby. Livestock teaches you responsibility and gives insight into how to care for those who need your aid in their lives.

As a senior in my retirement years, I cannot walk away from those things that have always filled my life with purpose and taught me life principles on many levels. Those who never have the opportunity to experience personal relationships with God's creation cannot grasp fully how they fill our lives on many levels.

www.ingramcontent.com/pod-product-compliance
Lightning Source LLC
Chambersburg PA
CBHW041544120125
20249CB00026B/1933